SPACE ROCKS

Written by David Rheinstrom and Jillian Schrager
Designed and Illustrated by Daniel Jankowski

Copyright © 2019 Scholastic Inc.

tangerine Press
an imprint of
■SCHOLASTIC
scholastic.com

Scholastic Inc., 557 Broadway, New York, NY 10012

10 9 8 7 6 5 4 3

ISBN: 978-1-338-17152-5

Printed in Guangzhou, China

CONTENTS

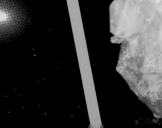

METEOR, METEOROID, OR METEORITE?

Some say it might be a meteor, others say it's a meteoroid, still OTHERS say it's a meteorite! What are those things, and what's the difference?

When that chunk of rock burns through the darkening sky, it gives off a bright flash of light.

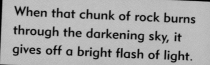

When it finally lands on Earth's crust, we call it a meteorite.

Keep it straight with this little rhyme!

A meteoroid is a rock out in space, many millions of miles from here. A meteor's when that rock starts to burn up, 'cause it's hitting Earth's atmosphere.

Remember:

'Roid is distant, meteors burn; 'rite's on the ground of Earth that turns.

WHEN SPACE GETS STINKY...

does it take a meteor shower?

NO.

In fact, a **meteor shower** is the opposite of clean. It happens when dust clouds, left behind from a comet's burning **tail**, crosses the path of Earth's orbit.

When this dust cloud hits Earth's atmosphere, it lights up in a beautiful, streaking display.

Some of these dust clouds are predictable, and Earth passes through them around the same time each year. Those dust clouds burn up when they enter the atmosphere, and we call that a *meteor shower*.

Though meteor showers come from comets, individual showers are named for the constellation they come from.

For example, the Perseid meteor shower (seen every August) appears to come from the constellation Perseus, whereas the Leonids (which have their peak in November) appear to come out of the constellation Leo.

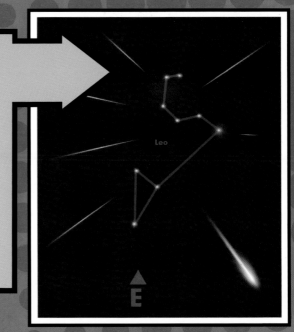

Every 33 years or so, Earth traverses a very dusty portion of the Leonid Cloud, resulting in a special meteor shower known as a **meteor storm!**

The Leonid meteor showers of 1833 and 1966 were two extraordinarily notable storms, with sightings of more than 150,000 to 200,000 meteor sightings an hour.

Accounts from that time describe the meteor storm as being like a snowstorm of light. Imagine making a snowman out of meteors!

ASTEROIDS!

Space rocks the size of city blocks

Most meteorites—in fact the overwhelming majority—come from **asteroids**, those enormous chunks of rock that hold orbit in the **asteroid belt** between Mars and Jupiter.

Asteroids are basically tiny planets—the remnants of the processes that created our solar system. Now, "tiny" is a relative term, here: there are about a million asteroids in the *asteroid belt* that are a half-mile (.8 km) or more in diameter. But if you rolled all of them into a ball, that ball would *still* weigh less than the moon.

Most of the remaining meteoroids that make their way toward Earth are pieces of lunar or Martian rock, dislodged by their own meteorite impacts.

Mars

Uranus

Mercury   Earth

Jupiter

Pluto

Neptune

Sun

Venus

Saturn

Asteroids bounce around in space—that's why they're so pitted and cratered—and those collisions send chunks flying in all directions. Those chunks … are meteoroids!

MOON

CERES

EARTH

The first-ever asteroid to be discovered by a human was the asteroid Ceres—587 mi. (945 km) in diameter, Ceres is the 33rd-largest object in the solar system. It's classified either as an asteroid or a dwarf planet (like Pluto). That's how big it is.

WHEN SPACE ATTACKS!

Asteroid Impact Events

Even though we may not see them, lots of very small asteroids pass by Earth every day. Most are just moving through our cosmic neighborhood, and don't even enter our atmosphere.

The asteroids that do enter the atmosphere are usually so small they burn up before they hit Earth. This is a process called **ablation**.

On very rare occasions, a larger asteroid will enter Earth's atmosphere, and it will be too big to slow down or burn up as it hurtles toward our planet. The collision that occurs when these asteroids hit Earth's surface is called a **hypervelocity impact**.

Hypervelocity impacts create bowl-shaped dents in the surface of the earth that we call **meteor craters**.

There are 190 identified meteor craters on Earth, and they range from just 317 ft. (97 m) across—a little smaller than a football field—to 186 mi. (299 km) across, which is about the size of Massachusetts.

Scientists believe that a massive impact from an asteroid or comet (like an asteroid, but icier) 66 million years ago drastically changed Earth's environment. They believe this resulted in the extinction of about 75 percent of all plants and animals on Earth, including the dinosaurs. This event is called the Cretaceous-Paleogene Extinction Event, because it marked the end of the Cretaceous and Paleogene eras.

TOP 5 COOLEST ASTEROID CRATERS ON EARTH

5 Vredefort Crater

Located in South Africa, the Vredefort Crater is both the oldest and the biggest crater on our list. The asteroid that created this massive structure would have been between 6 mi. (10 km) and 9 mi. (14 km) wide. Scientists believe it was created more than 2 billion years ago!

4 Karakul Crater

A deep lake in the mountains of Tajikistan, Karakul is the highest known impact crater: it's 12,990 ft. (3,959 m) above sea level. Its name means Black Lake. The crater is made up of two parts: one that is only about 62 ft. (19 m) deep, and another that goes 755 ft. (230 m) down into Earth's crust.

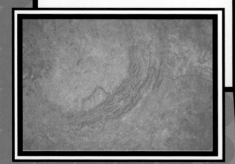

3 Deep Bay Crater

Deep Bay Crater, formed 99 million years ago, is near the edge of Reindeer Lake in Saskatchewan, Canada. This crater forms an unusually circular bay that is 8 mi. (13 km) across and about 720 ft. (219 m) deep, compared with the rest of the relatively shallow Reindeer Lake, which is only 56 ft. (17 m) deep.

2 Barringer Crater

Barringer Crater is named after Daniel Barringer, who lived from 1860 to 1929. He was the first geologist to hypothesize (make a scientific guess) about impact events on Earth. This desert crater is in Arizona, not too far from the Grand Canyon. It's almost a mile (1.6 km) across, 2 1/2 mi. (4 km) around, and 550 ft. (168 m) deep.

1 Chicxulub Crater

The Chicxulub Crater is on the Yucatan Peninsula in southeastern Mexico, about 600 mi. (966 km) directly south of New Orleans. It wasn't discovered until 1978 because it is impossible to see: it's buried under thousands of feet of limestone beneath the Caribbean Sea. So what makes this meteor crater special if we can't even see it?

Scientists believe the Chicxulub impact was responsible for the Cretaceous-Paleogene Extinction Event. The asteroid that caused this crater was a bolide, or meteorite fireball. This particular **bolide** was at least 6 mi. (10 km) across, and the crater it created is 110 mi. (177 km) wide and 12 mi. (19 km) deep. That makes Chicxulub the third-largest meteor crater on Earth and the absolute coolest on our list!

Craters don't just happen on Earth! They can occur on any object in space. In fact, the moon is covered in craters caused by meteors and asteroids, giving it its distinctive, Swiss-cheese look!

If you think Earth has some big craters, you should check out the South Pole-Aitken Basin on the moon. It's so big that you can even see it from Earth! Next time you're moon gazing, look for a big ring of mountains. That's the South Pole-Aitken Basin.

COMETS!

Where meteor showers come from!

Our solar system, like all solar systems, is a smushed-together collection of gases and stardust. Billions of years ago, scientists believe that stardust came together, heated up, and became the sun. Most of the leftover mass became the planets and asteroids, but at the very edge of our solar system, there's some mass that never condensed into anything especially large. There's a thing called the **Oort Cloud**; it's farther out than Pluto, and astronomers think most comets originate from it.

Far out from the sun, these gases and dust clouds froze into dense, dirty snowballs, whose orbits can be influenced by the movement of the planets.

Comets are DIRTY SPACE SNOWBALLS.

As comets loop through the solar system on their long orbital journeys, they leave bits of themselves behind.

This is why a comet has what's called a tail. It's made up of dust and gas, released when the comet flies near enough to the sun to start melting.

The word comet comes from the ancient Greek word for "hair." The philosopher Aristotle, seeing a comet's tail, described it as an *aster kometes*—a long-haired star!

DRAW THE GALAXY'S COOLEST COMET

A new and excellent
comet has just been
sighted for the first time!
What does it look like?

HALLEY'S COMET

A HISTORY

The most famous comet in history is undoubtedly Halley's Comet, named for the 18th-century English astronomer Edmond Halley. Halley figured out that the comet, which had been seen by humans since prehistoric times, arrived on a very predictable schedule every 75 to 76 years.

The earliest confirmed sighting of Halley's comet in history dates to 240 BCE, when a reference to a great comet appears in the *Shiji*, a history of Han Dynasty China.

In the past, people didn't know what to make of comets, but mostly they were afraid of them.

Most unexplained astrological events were usually thought of as bad omens. The full name for the flu, *influenza*, is Italian for *influence*; it refers to the belief that comets, meteors, or other space phenomena could cause illness.

In the year 1066 CE, Halley's Comet was seen as a terrible omen by the English and an especially bad omen for King Harald II. That omen came true later that year when the Norman French invaded and conquered England, and Harald was killed in the Battle of Hastings.

The comet appears in the Bayeux Tapestry, an enormous, 230 ft. (70 m) embroidery that tells the story of the Norman Conquest.

LET'S CRACK THIS THING OPEN!

You may have noticed by now that this book came with an odd-looking rock-type thing and a some tools.

LET'S USE 'EM!

HERE'S WHAT YOU'LL NEED

- Somewhere to bust up the rocks where you won't do damage to your home (so, not your grandma's glass coffee table)

- Permission from a grown-up

- Wooden chisel

- Wooden hammer

- The mysterious rock block that came with this book

Now... bust out from the dust and crack that sucker open! Get to excavating! There are rocks in that block!

WHAT TO DO

1. Spread out newspaper or an old towel on a flat surface.

2. Get your Space Rocks box and empty out all the contents. Punch out the clear acetate window too.

3. Place the box on the newspaper. Then place the rock block in the box.

Get some goggles on. We don't want any rock chips flying into your eyeballs.

4. Use your hammer and chisel to tap the block and loosen the hard dirt.

5. As pieces begin to break off, start searching for the mysterious rocks hidden inside.

6. Carve away excess dirt from around each rock using your chisel.

7. By the end of your excavation, you should find a total of four hidden rocks.

19

SPACE ROCK PROBE

Now it's time to dig a little deeper to see which rock has the greatest connection to outer space.

When a space rock hits Earth, geologists have the job of discovering what it's made of, which could be just about anything. Space rocks are composed of particles from all the celestial bodies they've come in contact with. That means a space rock that hits Earth could be composed of small parts of whatever is located on the ground where the space rock hits.

The fun is in discovering what's from Earth and what's from...

OUTER SPACE?

HERE'S WHAT YOU NEED FOR YOUR SPACE ROCK PROBE:

- Plastic cup from your UV display case
- A second cup or container
- Secret space reagent
- Distilled white vinegar
- Plastic scoop
- Plastic spoon
- Napkins or paper towels
- Scissors
- Somewhere to bust up the rocks where you won't do damage to your home (so, not your grandma's glass coffee table)

WARNING: This experiment requires scissors. Adult helper needed.

A reagent is a substance that causes another substance to reveal its makeup by how it reacts when the two are combined. In this case, your reagent is baking soda.

WHAT TO DO:

1. Fill the plastic cup half-way with distilled white vinegar.

2. Have an adult help you cut open the bag of secret space reagent.

3. Pour all of the reagent into the second cup or container.

4. Drop any one of the rocks into the cup with the vinegar.

5. Wait about 10 seconds.

6. Use the scoop to scoop out some of the reagent and pour it into the cup with the rock and the vinegar.

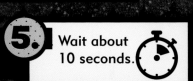

7. Watch the reaction. What do you observe?

8. Use the plastic spoon to fish out the rock and place it on a napkin or paper towel.

9. Use the napkin or paper towel to dry the rock.

10. Repeat these steps for all the rocks.

Flip to the next page to see what kind of rocks you've unearthed.

ROCKIN' IN THE FREE WORLD

What did you find?

CALCITE A carbonate mineral that fizzes when exposed to acid and glows under UV light! Could it be… *FROM OUTER SPACE?*

TEKTITE A kind of glass formed when a meteorite hits Earth's surface! Could it be… *FROM OUTER SPACE?*

Are any of these rocks VISITORS FROM OUTER SPACE?

Well, no. Technically.

But let us tell you why these rocks are still awesome.

See, when a meteoroid enters Earth's atmosphere, becoming a meteor, and strikes Earth's crust, becoming—you guessed it—a meteorite, sometimes it hits really hard. This impact causes sand and rock to *melt*, tossing it high up into the air.

GREEN SERPENTINE (ANTIGORITE)

A kind of rock which, when it gets into water and soil, is toxic to plants. Could it be…

FROM OUTER SPACE?

SLATE

A chemically inert, flameproof mineral. Could it be… you know what? Probably not, right?

Some tektites, such as australite, were ejected so high into the atmosphere that they hardened and melted again as they came down to Earth, giving them their weird, button-like shape.

So what you're holding, when you hold a tektite, is the *result* of a meteorite or asteroid striking Earth. We would have gotten you an asteroid, but it wouldn't have fit in the book.

Well, okay, fine. But what's the deal with the glowy rock? Is *that* from space?

IT'S JUST FLUORESCENT

But what does *that* mean?

GOOD QUESTION!

First of all, there are many different kinds of light. Light is a kind of radiation that we can see. There's also light we *can't* see, such as microwaves, infrared, or ultraviolet.

If you shine a flashlight at a mirror, you'll see that light reflected back at you. If you shined a UV flashlight at that same mirror, you'd see nothing.

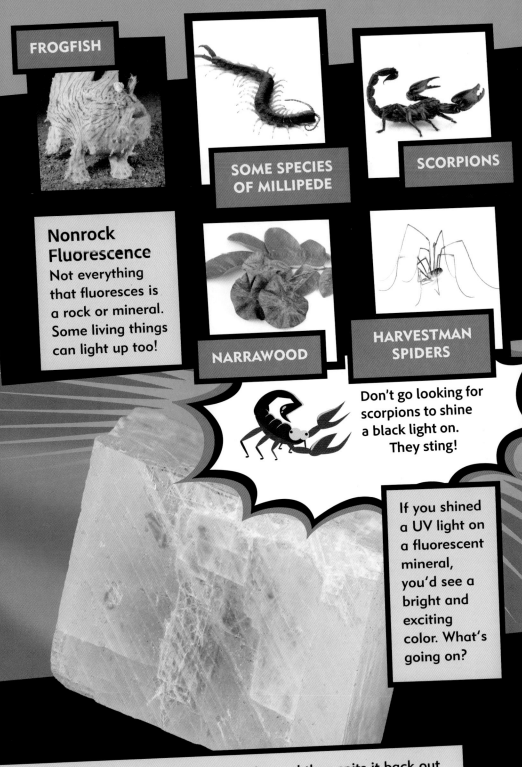

FROGFISH

SOME SPECIES
OF MILLIPEDE

SCORPIONS

Nonrock
Fluorescence
Not everything
that fluoresces is
a rock or mineral.
Some living things
can light up too!

NARRAWOOD

HARVESTMAN
SPIDERS

Don't go looking for
scorpions to shine
a black light on.
They sting!

If you shined
a UV light on
a fluorescent
mineral,
you'd see a
bright and
exciting
color. What's
going on?

The glowing object absorbs the UV light, and then spits it back out
at a lower frequency, making it possible for your eyes to detect it.

EVERYDAY FLUORESCENCE

Today's greatest minds use glow technology!

Fluorescent Lighting

Where are you right now? Library? School? There's a good chance the ceiling lights above you are fluorescent. Inside a fluorescent light bulb an electrical discharge produces ultraviolet light; the inside of the light bulb is coated with a special type of fluorescent paint that reacts to the UV rays, and it produces visible light. Fluorescent lighting is an energy saver, lasts longer than a regular light bulb, and keeps cooler.

Forensics

If you've ever watched a cop show, then you've probably seen fluorescence in action. The police and **forensic** investigator sprays a fluorescent chemical on the surface they are studying. This chemical highlights traces of invisible **DNA** material and helps them discover what happened.

Optical Brighteners

Paper and fabric manufacturers use fluorescent compounds called optical brighteners to brighten their products so they'll look white, bright, and crisp. **Optical brighteners** are also used on glow-in-the-dark strips on bike helmets, jackets, and backpacks so they can be seen at night. An ingredient in laundry detergent, optical brighteners are used to keep your white clothes looking clean and new.

SHOW OFF THAT GLOW!

Use the UV light display in your kit to show off your fluorescent rock!

 Before you use the UV display case, have an adult help you install the batteries. Refer to the back of the book for battery information, if you need assistance.

1. Place the clear plastic cup of your UV display case on a flat surface.

2. Put the fluorescent rock, calcite, in the cup.

3. Secure the top of the case onto the cup.

4. Turn on the switch located on the top of the display case.

5. Turn off all the lights in the room. Make it as dark as possible.

WHAT DO YOU SEE?

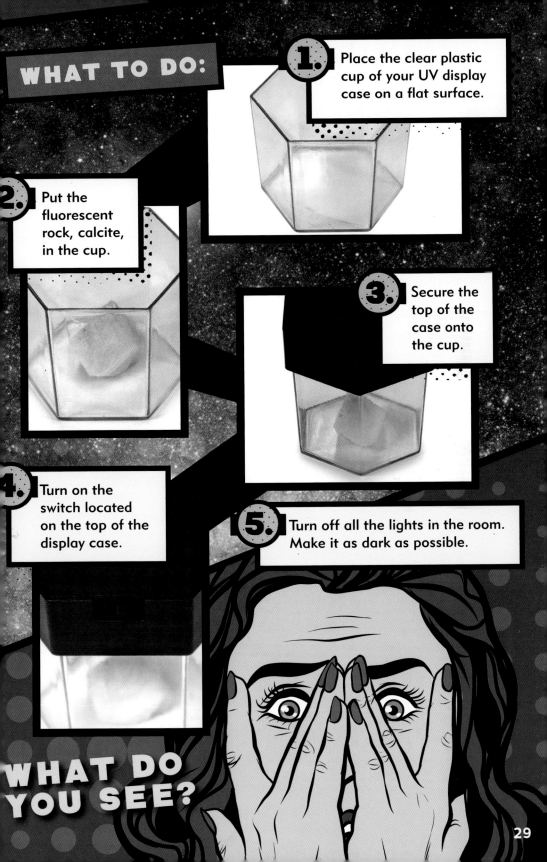

THE TRUTH COMES OUT

WE FIGURED OUT WHAT THAT UNIDENTIFIED OBJECT WAS.

The mysterious object turned out to be calcite, a common Earth mineral with curious properties. Despite the terrestrial origin of this mineral, could it be that the glowy part comes from...

being cursed by an alien?

THE WORLD MAY NEVER KNOW.

GLOSSARY

ablation – occurs when a meteoroid flies into Earth's atmosphere and it gets very hot. As it burns, it begins to vaporize and burn away.

asteroid belt – the part of the solar system between Mars and Jupiter that is full of chunks of space-rock called asteroids

asteroids – rocky objects found in the inner solar system (between Jupiter and Mars; also known as minor planets)

bolide – a larger-than-normal meteor that burns very brightly as it enters Earth's atmosphere; some bolides can be seen in the daytime!

celestial bodies – any object in space, such as a comet, a planet, or a meteoroid

DNA – short for DeoxyriboNucleic Acid; contains the genetic material (or blueprint) for every living thing and how it is supposed to look and act

forensics – the science of solving crimes

hypervelocity impact – when a celestial object collides with the earth at a speed of 6,700 mph (10,783 km) or faster

meteor – an object that burns brightly as it enters Earth's atmosphere

meteor craters – a big dent that is formed when a meteor or an asteroid hits it

meteor shower – a brilliant display of tiny, burning dust particles that regularly enter Earth's atmosphere when its orbit intersects with the dusty path of a comet

meteor storm – a brighter-than-usual meteor shower

meteorite – a meteor that has survived its trip through Earth's atmosphere without completely burning up, and has landed on the ground

meteoroid – a rocky object in space, smaller than an asteroid

Oort Cloud – a frosty gas cloud from which comets originate; believed to be far out, beyond Neptune

optical brighteners – chemicals used to make products look brighter

tail – the trail of gas, plasma, and space dust that a comet leaves behind

SAFETY INFORMATION

This kit comes with the following components:

- 32-page Space Rocks activity book
- Brush
- Wooden hammer
- Wooden chisel
- Plastic scoop
- Pouch of secret space reagent*
- Mysterious rock**
- 4 hidden rocks
- UV light display case

IMPORTANT:
Before you dig into your kit, read the safety and product information in this user's guide.

* *Baking soda*
** *Digging block is made of pottery clay, water, and gypsum.*

ALWAYS ASK AN ADULT BEFORE YOU BEGIN.

- Get an adult's permission before performing the digging activity in this kit.
- Do not perform the experiments in the book using equipment that is not supplied with the kit or recommended in the book.
- Wash your hands before and after you perform the digging activity.
- Keep the activity area clean and away from food storage. The activity area should be well-lit, ventilated, and close to a water supply.
- The digging activity will kick up fine particles. Protect your eyes, nose, and mouth while performing the activity. Wear goggles and a mask.
- Keep food and drinks away from your activity area. Do not eat or drink while performing the activity. Do not place materials associated with this product in your mouth.
- Some experiments will require you to use common household objects. Be sure to ask an adult before you use any of these items.
- To avoid breakage, dig and brush gently to extract the rocks.
- When you are done with the activity in this kit, store the components away immediately.
- Clean the activity area immediately after performing the activity.
- Do not dispose of the plaster debris and powder down the drain. Put the material into a plastic bag. Then seal the bag and throw it into the trash.
- This kit and its finished product contain small parts. Improper usage may be a choking hazard. Keep product away from pets and young children.
- If you have any allergic reactions to the product, seek medical advice right away. Take the product with you.

Warning Regarding Baking Soda

- Do not inhale the baking soda. Avoid prolonged exposure to skin. Avoid contact with eyes. In case of contact with eyes, rinse with plenty of water and seek immediate medical advice. If baking soda is swallowed, seek medical advice right away. Take the product and packaging with you.
- Baking soda may stick, making it difficult to remove. So avoid contact with hair, carpets, and fabric.
- Do not put baking soda or the items made with the baking soda down the drain. Put the baking soda and items into a plastic bag, seal the bag, and then throw them in the trash.
- Store baking soda in a well-ventilated place. Avoid direct exposure to sunlight. Do not put baking soda in a windy area.